21 Love Letters To Myself

Vaishna Raj

BookLeaf Publishing

India | USA | UK

Made with ❤ on the BookLeaf Publishing Platform
www.bookleafpub.in
www.bookleafpub.com

Dedication

Do you find yourself, lost in the web of monotony, caught up in the process of life, yet forgetting to live,to love, to laugh and to lighten up sometimes? Then, this book is dedicated for you, my reader.Yes, you are reading this book at the right time, in the right space and for the right reason!

Preface

After putting down papers for the first job I signed up for and after losing someone I love, The world felt bleak and uncertain. But as there is a saying which goes, 'After the darkest hour of the night, you will find the light''. It is when I decided to jot down my thoughts in a book. When I first started writing the book, I had no idea what the book would look like. A tidal wave of thoughts, hit by a wave of self doubt and anxiety, one day I decided to be the love letter to myself. That's when '21 Letters to Myself' came into life.

In this book, you can find poems with self realisations, affirmations and a roller coaster of emotions. This book will serve as the catharsis of emotions you have always craved for, it can serve as your secret diary to be kept in your pocket or your backpack. This book will also be your best friend & your Self-care Journal during days of turbulence.

Acknowledgements

To all the people I have let go of and have let go of me.
To all the souls, whom I love and who love me so much.
To all the poets, artists, and lives who have inspired me.
To all the dreams, places and moments,
 I have chased, chasing and still continue to do so..
A big 'Thank you'
This book is for you.

The Art of Letting Go

When I stand here,
taking with me a heap of collected memories in a tiny
bottle!
When I stand here,
counting the times I have told myself,
I would not be able to hold the freedom,
which I have been showering myself with, lately!
When I stand here,
Being grateful for the connections, I have mended over
the years.
When I stand here ,
trying to measure the disparity of the city and the slums
When I stand here,
questioning myself, for finding a middle ground among
the chaos!
When I stand here,
trying to redefine what chaos means to me.
Lost Love, Given up dreams and those golden butterflies
in my belly!
First Love, First Bestfriend, First Job..

Left Pieces of Myself with a few.
And Have become an archive of them too.
This is where it all began!
Love for sunflowers, dream catchers and handwritten letters!
Heart pounding like tribal drum beats,
For Jhumkas, noserings and poetry!
Places, People, Passion
I have let go of and have let go of me!
Miles to go before I sleep!
Miles I have come, trusting myself.
And miles which I can never even reach
Taking a clutch of guilty,
Rubbing my eyes like wilted petals
and muting my inner speech,
I stand still !
Trying to feel and immerse myself in this very moment
Do we all live for moments like these?

Grief

Grief, it is what it is!
Holding a cup of coffee, wiping my sweat with a lace hanky,
gazing through the window pane!
Feeling the raindrops!
Feeling stuck in my body!
The Neverending loop of the mental movie playing in my head.
Wish I had given it a second thought,
before jumping into it.
Wish I had ended it properly.
Wish I can go back and start from the scratch?
Also wish I can skip this and create a new reality?
The magic dust has faded...
Days filled with darkness..
Embracing the void.
And inside my head,
there is a teeny tiny voice ,
which keeps murmuring to me,
This is where it all begins..

The taste of detachment!
The taste of freedom!
No longer obliged to anyone or anything.
No longer held back.
The outspokenness has taken a pause
The urge to create new experiences feels monotonous.
Running into someone's arms for help, feels meaningless...
And being in your head feels restrictive..
Let me be the wind.
Let me be this moment.
Let me disappear for once...
Let me blend with the world and become unrecognizable for a while?
Let me lose my voice and give all to the world?
Let me feel my silence and at the same time,
capture all the laughs, the voices, the happy eyes, the shimmering skin
And let me be me...
And I am letting it go
To the fine air.....!!!

Healing

The cold breeze.
The dusty evenings.
The caressing lips.
The way my fingers glided over the glass door.
My eyes glued to the sight inside!
How my breath caught in my throat.
Bouts of nostalgia hitting me like a bucket of cold water
Sometimes I wonder,
Should I be happy that I have healed my past
Or should I be sad that I have outgrown my dream
After all, memories warp and woof the fabric called self
right?
But that night, when the clock struck 11 pm, all I could
hold onto was nothingness
One more hour for the New Year!
But separation is good, right?
No more attached to anything, which used to bother me
for so long
I feel free, tender and subtle
In that case, may I rephrase the line?

I did not hold onto nothingness
I was in fact experiencing the tremendous fullness
A proper closure
A December feeling it was!
Now I get it!
'Perspective'
And a beautiful December night gave way to the first light of New Year.

Smile

On days, when I hardly know, what to speak, I smile!
I smile a lot these days!
Oh my dear Smile!
I have been in love with you since forever.
I owe you!
Happiness is my ignorance, they say!
Like a lotus unwrapping from its bud
Smile has become my emotion!
Does performativity subtly reside within?
Neither have they had a faded notion of why I smile a lot
these days
Nor do they know how much I crave for the right words.
Things are not the same anymore!
The melancholy dressed like sunshine
The Chaos, subtly arranged in a box
The hands of a giver, they are!
That is all who I am!
Oh my dear smile!
Do not leave me for I would be lost without your wild
touch,

without knowing how to hold my lips and hide my words anymore!

Telling myself how to get up everytime with a smile has become my favourite hobby so far.

. Boundless, untamed & liberated

A metaphor of butterflies and flowers,
That's all who I am
The more you try to hold me tight,
I'll either wither or take flight.
But even those withered flowers,
And butterflies that flutter away,
Will stay, when they feel
Their beauty's not questioned,
nor obsessed with,
But simply accepted as it is.
Haven't you seen butterflies on flowers?
Fluttering their wings to engineer the world..
Is it because both are free like a breeze,
Never obliged to anything,
But wanting to be for each other—
Held closely, but not tightly?
Let us go wild and free,

Let us get lost in the Chaos..
And never come back even for once..!

When I got my first tatto

The whole february drenched in spring and love letters.
Why not get one for myself?
The bangalore, flowered with the Bougainvillea, sunflowers,
And Pink trumpet trees all over..
The smell of hope.
The evening was hazy,
Melancholy embracing my finger tips,
reaching my shoulder!
And embracing each and every bit of my body
Painting an elegy, That's all I wanted.
Received two notifications,
As always, I didn't want to settle for less any more.
Even though I craved for it, in mind deeply,
I held onto nothingness.
And that became my strength!
And that's what my love letter looks like!
Drenched in Love,
Got my first tattoo, the Sunflower in its full glory
Sunflower, showering the unwavering faith!

While the loop of uncertainties bounce back..
The way my body felt powerful,
When the liner needle moved across my shoulder,
Marking the comeback!
All I could see was a mirage.
And please let me hold onto it for once.
And let this february be a forever memory!

When I quit my first Job

The thought lingered near, ever-present,
Clouding me in all the walks of life,
Leaving behind all the lost dreams,
Hope, and sleepless nights.
It felt hard to come back to myself at times.
It felt as if I had been pretending,
That I didn't know myself for the past two years.
The time has come.
The time to put an end to staying numb,
The time to stop embracing my ignorance.
The times felt turbulent,
The world felt bleak.
Yet, a few people, very few,
Seemed quite supportive.
The decision was not easy,
Yet it was made.
Taking a pause after the past 24 years,
Looking back for the first time,
Pondering whether my future self would ever be proud
of me,

*If I didn't choose to stop leaning into the loop again and
again.
A loop of uncertainty,
Dressed in hopes and dreams.
That's what it is!
So brave of me, to have taken the step,
And yet, I wait for the moment,
When I'll unveil into my beautiful version.*

Golden Void

For the first time in my life,
I am not running away,
From my shattered dreams and thoughts.
Pausing just a little,
Taking that unknown, long road,
Creates a chaos of confusion,
Hopelessness, sadness, fragility, and fear.
It pushes you into a void,
Which I would call the golden void.
I know, it doesn't sound "golden,"
Nor does it sprinkle magic dust
Into your tummy.
But it makes your boat burn,
And you lose yourself,
If you don't move.
But this is where I would like to begin my journey!
Perhaps, aren't we all in the same boat?

Hope

There are some days,
You feel so lost,
You don't know what you like,
Don't know what you dislike,
And you're not in the space
To figure out what's right for you.
There are some days,
You don't feel like getting up from your bed,
You feel the world is moving fast,
That you're left behind,
That you're not enough,
And that you've outgrown your interests,
Habits, relations, and desires.
But have you listened to that teeny-tiny voice inside,
Which still whispers,
"It's okay. I got this."
Yes, Hope.
The hope that I'll figure it out, along the way,
The hope that I can let go of my past,
And hold onto my loved ones, without doubt,

The hope that even if I outgrow my relations,
I can make better ones.
The hope that my primary circle of friends
Would be my home forever,
The hope that my family would love me,
And be there for me forever.
The hope that even if things don't work out the way I want,
There are better things coming.
The hope that even if better things don't happen to me,
It would be okay.
The hope that I am more than all of this.
Do you believe in intuitions?
Do you believe in miracles?
Do you believe in faith?
Or do you think they are all stupid lies
That we've been telling ourselves all this while?

The Feeling of Outgrowing

I always outgrow people,
A tendency woven deep within me,
Yet it's never as simple as it seems—
Like trying to arrange chaos in a box.
Guilt lingers,
A constant companion.
When loneliness settles in,
I meet someone close,
And in that moment,
I realize—
I have outgrown.
The bond remains.
The love persists.
But the language I speak has shifted.
And so, I find myself in a place
Where 'strangers' start to feel like home,
For they know nothing of me,
And I no longer belong there.
Slowly, you begin to seek comfort
In 'detachment' from connection.

In other words,
You find yourself more connected to your own soul.
But here, growth unfolds.
Yet not all relationships fade.
You outgrow those
Not aligned with your growth,
Not in tune with your phase—
Maybe. Or maybe not.
I can't say for sure.
But one thing I know,
This feeling is 'new.'
And I am learning to embrace it.

The City Life

The breeze caressed the swaying green leaves,
Carrying the fragrance of lush mango limbs,
And the melodious song of the cuckoo within.
It stole a glance through the window pane of my room,
Playing hide and seek through my flickering eyelashes.
The concept of "city life"
Has always given me goosebumps.
I had always imagined living in a city—
Forced conversations,
A lot of learning and unlearning,
Some performative relations.

But rather than feeling tired,
There's something in me
That draws me to this 'ambiguity.'
Is it the feeling of escape
That comes when you realize
You don't have to be yourself for a while?

Cocoon of Realisation

Cranberries..
Related to blueberries and wintergreen,
But never quite one of them.
Taste comprises both sour and bitter.
Sometimes,
The energy or frequency cannot be put in a box,
Maybe because it's meant to stand out!
Maybe I am picky,
In terms of what I want from life.
How my pupils dilated,
When they touched the yellow lights,
How they cherished the sunflowers in my belly!
How my eyelashes spoke to my eyes...
I felt seen and heard.
It is not a void—
Rather, it is a cocoon,
A cocoon of mental peace and realization.

First Panic Attack

I wish you had known,
That you would survive this, as you always do.
I still remember that night—
It felt dark, so bleak, so true.
That night,
When the world came to a standstill,
When breath escaped, so long,
And everything felt subtle, hard, and wrong.
The faded memory of how the body felt,
It wasn't anger, the face not red,
It wasn't sadness, for the eyes held instead
A secret deep, where emotions dwell.
My heartbeats were like tribal drums,
And voices crackled, the silence hums.
Forty-five minutes—just that brief,
And then I saw—
It was a rebirth, a new belief.
From that moment, I began to see,
That miracles are born,
In places dark, like you and me.

First Bouquet

With a tint of December feeling,
Added to a pinch of thick climate,
Like a tang of ice on my lips,
And a hint of pine, which felt like
A walk of green, a walk of silence,
And a walk to remember...
As usual, my friend kept telling me,
That I look pretty,
And he wanted to confess something.
I still remember the moondust in my lungs,
When he said that.
And we both, as usual,
After getting a mug of hot chocolate,
Walked through the Bangalore streets,
Looking at the busy world outside.
It felt good to see so much happening,
Alive instances, people lost in their own worlds.
He asked me to close my eyes,
And when I opened them,
I saw a huge bouquet of flowers—

White ones, red ones, and violet ones.
My heart danced to the tunes of the breeze outside,
My body felt tired, yet wonderful at the same time.
My mind, my eyelashes, my body—
Beating to the feeling,
The feeling of love...
For the first time,
Someone gifted me a beautiful bouquet,
One that felt serene,
One that touched my heart.
It felt as if the rain had poured down onto my belly,
Such an undefinable feeling,
Yet so beautifully real.

My Long distance Friend

The friend is still close to my heart,
Though words between us now fall apart.
Like a fantasy that came alive,
She appeared on a dark, uncertain night,
When I wasn't sure I could survive.

She was the only one I could turn to,
When the world felt cold and askew,
Far from home, from family's embrace,
As if the world had turned its face.
I hid in my room, lost in despair,
That's when she found me, standing there.

She met my soft, unhealed side,
My gentle, tender heart, open wide.
And loved me, flaws and all,
Her love unshaken, standing tall.

Being a Malayali girl,
It felt like discovering another world.

She was from Jammu, full of grace,
But I called her "Kashmiri Apple" with a smile on my
face.
Her cheeks would blush, red with delight,
Each laugh carried a sense of hope
To sail throughout.

In her, I learned the art of love,
Of friendship, kindness, from above.
The strength of softness, the power to be,
To stand tall, and yet still be free.
The lessons I learned from her
I carry along the walks of life,
Grateful for my university days,
Never a day has passed without gratitude,
For the wonder she brought into my world.
And long I have come, With her lessons, always near.

To my Younger Self

I wish that you knew,
It was never your fault,
You're allowed to embrace life's richness,
For you are beautiful, and strong in every way.

You deserve love,
You deserve joy,
You are sensitive, and that's what makes you shine,
Quite adorable, uniquely divine.

It was never about being the topper,
Nor the trendsetter, nor the crowd's applause,
It was never about popularity or being cool—
It was always you, your heart, your dreams, your soul.

I wish that you knew,
Ten years from now, none of this will matter,
The struggles you face will be faded chatter.

You'll hold a self-image, radiant and true,

And people's opinions will no longer matter to you..
With self-love and compassion in your heart,
You'll cherish yourself, right from the start.

You've got it all, my love,
You've always had it inside.
So, embrace the journey—
With your heart open wide.

To my Future Self

Ten years from now,
I promise, darling,
You'll have all that you've asked for,
The tears in your eyes will be no more.
Everything you've dreamed of is on its way,
Just hold on, stay calm, come what may.
Your dream career, life, and soulmate,
Are just two steps away—don't hesitate.
Just because you don't have it now,
Doesn't mean it won't come to you somehow.
This is just a phase,
And you are meant to outshine, always.
Because you are, and always will be,
The most beautiful soul for all to see.
You believe, and that's your light,
A bowl of sunshine shining bright.
Mixed with apple pine, sweet as honey,
Showering moon dust, soft and sunny.
You, my love, are just phenomenal—
Hitting the rock bottom,

Facing the fall,
Rising up like a phoenix bird,
Like a Catapult,
Working at high speed,
Chasing your dreams
And now the world is yours, my darling!

To my Present Self

Things have been a little hard lately,
The times feel uncertain,
Hardly know what to hope for,
Hardly know how to hold things anymore.
Hardly know what to hold onto,
And never a day passes
Without the very thought of how to figure this out.
As every dark cloud has a silver lining,
The day awaits,
The day to weave the fabric,
The fabric of dreams,
Chasing the self,
Billowing the white curtains of peace and love.
The sorrows are going to fade,
Awaiting a better tomorrow.

First Love

The cold breeze,
The dusty evenings,
The caressing lips,
How he played with my hair—
It was showering cats and dogs in my belly,
And the feeling tickled me all over.

The butterfly kisses, the glancing looks,
How he held my hand and never let me go.
We didn't speak—
It was pure silence,
It tasted like marshmallows,
Warm and fluffy,
Soft and sweet,
Calm through the chaos.

My body, a melancholic dream,
And the depth in your eyes,
Painting my elegy into a sonnet.

Core

It was always hard for me to decide what I like,
Caught in a loop of confusion, I'd think for hours,
And after days of fret and pondering,
Sorting out what I don't like became my favorite thing.
I hated summers, speed, and spiders,
Hated breaks, one-word texts, and the color 'pink.'
I hated the word 'obsession,'
And the sound of crickets at night,
The dogs' fur disturbed me, yet Jhumkas excited me.
I admired poetry, sunflowers, and tattoos,
Couldn't understand why people praised coffee over Chai,
Why friendship and love had to be different,
And why attachment and connection felt the same.
I fell in love with nose rings, mails, and port wine,
Fell in love too easily, and never truly fell out.
But I never stayed anywhere too long—
What a paradox, I've come to be.

A Liminal Space

After days of monotony and chaos,
I felt something deep and undefinable yesterday.
Fell in love with the streets I wandered,
And not the stores.
While the world seemed a bit busy,
I was on cloud nine when the heavy downpour came.
All drenched in rain,
Eavesdropping on what the rain was humming to the leaves,
The breeze that stole a glance at me,
The stranger who smiled at me.
The ten orange ice candies,
A conversation with my loved ones,
Who let me be me.
The ash-colored tall mounds in the sky,
The cacophony of noises from the auto rickshaw walas—
The world was speaking to me,
"Just pause for a moment."
I felt like holding on to time,
And never letting it go, for once.

What if clocks stopped ticking,
People stopped moving,
And the raindrops stayed in the air,
And the ice candy never melted?
A liminal space,
Where time stood still,
And I was just living.